D0190827

Please renew or return items by the date shown on your receipt

www.hertsdirect.org/libraries

Renewals and enquiries: 0300 123 4049

Textphone for hearing or speech impaired   0300 123 4041

First published in 2013 by Dalesman

an imprint of

Country Publications Ltd

The Water Mill, Broughton Hall

Skipton, North Yorkshire BD23 3AG

www.dalesman.co.uk

Text © Mike Pannett & Alan Wilkinson 2013

Photographs © John Potter 2013

ISBN 978-1-85568-312-9

Printed in China by 1010 Printing International Ltd.

Foreword

When I was a young man I decided that I fancied a career as a policeman. I applied, naturally enough, to join the North Yorkshire force. This was, after all, where I'd grown up. I knew the area – both its towns and its countryside – and I knew the people, the culture of my particular part of God's Own Country. I would be the perfect fit, surely.

So I wasn't happy when they turned me down. Nothing wrong with my attitude, my intelligence or fitness, nor my general aptitude. They made that quite plain. It was just that I wore glasses.

Fortunately for me, the Metropolitan Police weren't so choosy. I packed my bags, took the train to London and served there for ten years. And, looking back, perhaps it was for the best that I learned my trade in the capital. Because when I came home to Yorkshire in 1998 I was immediately struck by the fact that just to work in this part of the world was a huge privilege.

I was stationed at Malton. My patch, Ryedale, embraced 600 square miles of the most beautiful landscapes the county has to offer. Imagine patrolling the streets of Battersea and Clapham, then coming home to a beat that took in The North York Moors, the Yorkshire Wolds, and the Vale of York.

As I've written in the *Now Then, Lad* series, many a working day would begin with a drive through the Howardian Hills and up past Castle Howard. Or I might have to go up onto the Moors to investigate an incident at Kirbymoorside or Hutton-le-Hole. Other days I'd take my patrol car onto the Wolds at Birdsall, braking as I passed a string of racehorses trooping home from their exercises on the gallops. On the way back to town I might find myself pulling over to let the Middleton hounds come by. When it was time for a break I might park up on Sutton Bank, above the white horse, and enjoy one of the finest views in all of England. Do you wonder that I sometimes found myself chuckling, to think that I was being paid for this by the hour.

If working in Ryedale was a delight and a privilege, then being asked to compile this book is a real honour. When the photographer John Potter asked me for a list of the places that feature in the books – places where I'd chased poachers and burglars, investigated incidents involving wildlife, or gone out to join the search for missing hikers – I told him to brace himself. It would be quite a list. I think it ran to fourteen pages. It has taken John a full year, seeking out those very specific locations and waiting for ideal conditions. Occasionally he invited me to join him as he compiled a set of pictures which truly do justice to this great piece of country.

North Yorkshire has a place deep in my heart. I love it for its natural beauty, for the diversity of its landscape, for the space and solitude I find there – and also for the characters it produces, the warmth of the welcome I receive in the tea-shops, the village pubs, the market-places. But I don't think you need me to persuade you that this is a special, a wonderful place. So I'll be on my way, and leave you to enjoy the pictures.

contents

my "Patch"

North York Moor

River

Ros...

Rievaulx Abbey

Helmsley

THIRSK

Sutton Bank

Harrogate

YORK

map illustration by Christine Jopling ··· www.christinejopling.com

Getting to Know my Patch

As a rural beat copper I never knew what to expect when I went out on patrol. I might find myself involved in a high-speed car chase along the A64. I might have to visit a family in the wake of some domestic tragedy, or I might end up having a cup of tea and a slice of home-made cake as some farmer told me about the strangers with dogs he'd spotted in his fields after the sun had gone down. One way or another, my job involved the accumulation of a lot of information, and I valued the time I had to absorb it, and think it over. So I had my favourite spots where I'd park up, get out my notebook and think things over.

When I first returned North I lived up the hill here, above Leavening. No matter what else is happening, I only have to lean on this gate, looking across the Vale of York towards the distant Pennines, and my mood lifts.

Mike Pannett's Yorkshire

Leavening (left) lies at the foot of the Wolds, and on a chilly winter's day you're assured of a warm welcome at the Jolly Farmers (above), which lies at the heart of the village. I've had some great times there with the characters who feature in my books: Algy, Walter, and Soapy. He was the one who fixed the clock and had me drinking beer way past closing time. It's all in *Now Then, Lad*.

Above: I've occasionally tucked myself away out of sight in this stand of beech trees. From there you can look to all points of the compass.

A spot like Leavening Brow gives you a commanding view of the countryside. As the winter sun disappears to the south-west I've frequently spotted a flickering light across the stubble-fields as poachers get to work.

Right: My base: Malton 'nick'. Plenty of people drive past it the first time; they assume it's some posh person's house.

My Roots

I doubt that many people choose to spend their leisure time in what is actually their working environment. But what could be better than a day out in North Yorkshire? One of my favourite trips is to Staintondale, just north of Scarborough. I spent most of childhood holidays on a farm there, playing in the woods, running down to the waterfall at Hayburn Wyke (facing page, inset) and larking about on the beach (top). The big rock is where I caught my first codling. When we were all little, Mum and Dad would treat us to fish and chips in town, but later on we'd have Sunday lunch at the Hayburn Wyke Inn (above), a place I still visit with my wife to enjoy a pint of real ale. If you're coming to Yorkshire, can I recommend that you try one of the many beers and ales specially brewed by the Black Sheep Brewery in Masham.

You Never Know Where You'll End Up

Once night falls in an area as sparsely populated as ours, you can learn a lot just by sitting and watching for the lights of any vehicles on the move (right).

At its far northern end, my Ryedale beat reached almost to the coast. In the other direction we patrolled right up to the York bypass. The distance spanning the two extremes adds up to around forty miles. In fact, one of my first arrests took place, off-duty, in York's main shopping street. From to time my colleagues and I would have a night out in York – and of course we celebrated Soapy's stag night doing the legendary 'Micklegate run' – just through the Bar Walls there (below).

Among the more unusual places my work took me was the gun room at Wintringham (top right). This is where Hugh Cholmley (pictured right) and I got together and planned campaigns for my Country Watch members.

Facing page:

The A64 Malton bypass, otherwise known as the Crime Corridor. It was our senior management team who came up with the term 'Crime Corridor'. It sounds a lot more exciting than the plain old Malton bypass, and of course we coppers adopted it straight away – albeit with our tongues planted firmly in our cheeks.

I've had a few high-speed chases along this stretch of the bypass, and would regularly park up on the bridge here late at night to see who – or what – was coming through.

The fact is that the road offers a handy way into the maze of country roads that criss-cross Ryedale, connecting dozens of small communities. For drivers looking to make a fast getaway from the scene of a crime it offers rapid access to York, from where they can get onto the A1. And once they're there it's much harder to trace them. They can go anywhere: north, south or into the West Riding and across the Pennines.

When it comes to a high-speed pursuit – like the one described in *Not On My Patch, Lad* – your main objective is to try and stay on the suspect's tail. All that business of racing past them and forcing them off the roads – that's for Hollywood, and they're welcome to it. We're not in the business of endangering lives – especially our own.

I've written extensively about the activities of my Country Watch members. This is where we first met, in the Dawnay Arms in West Heslerton (right). I remember going along, wondering whether anybody would show up. I was greeted by over thirty members of the community, all willing to give up their time – sometimes at dead of night – to combat rural crime.

I hadn't been at Malton very long when I got a call to say that a couple of students had 'borrowed' a boat and were dangerously close to the weir at Kirkham (main image). It turned out they were celebrating their graduation.

The break-in at Ganton Golf Club (right) was more or less routine. Far more memorable was the time I ended up crawling across the eighteenth green in search of paw-prints that may – or may not – have been left by the 'Ryedale panther'.

The Moors are dotted with these ancient crosses. When the weather closes they're our most reliable landmarks. In *Not On My Patch, Lad* you can read how Ana Cross, pictured here, served as a vital reference point when we were searching for a lost hiker.

The great thing about being a copper is you can 'investigate' anything that seems unusual – like the sign at the Malt Shovel in Hovingham (above), or the stained-glass window (right) in Sand Hutton Church (facing page).

It's 'Grin' up North

There's a lot of fun in police work. Some of the criminals are regular comedians, and some of their 'jobs' are more like comic capers. We never caught the person who stole the Colonel's balls from the top of his gateway (right), but I do know that when he replaced them – at considerable expense – he made sure they were impossible to shift. Somehow, the colonel seemed to attract out-of-the-ordinary criminals. The last time I called on him he'd been having trouble with someone nicking milk off his front doorstep.

Sometimes your casework can follow you on a night out. In that sense, you're always on duty. The time Ann and I went on a ghost walk in York, who should pop out of the shadows to add colour to our guide's talk but that well-known local villain Ronnie Leach, dressed up as a ghostly 'extra' at ten quid a night.

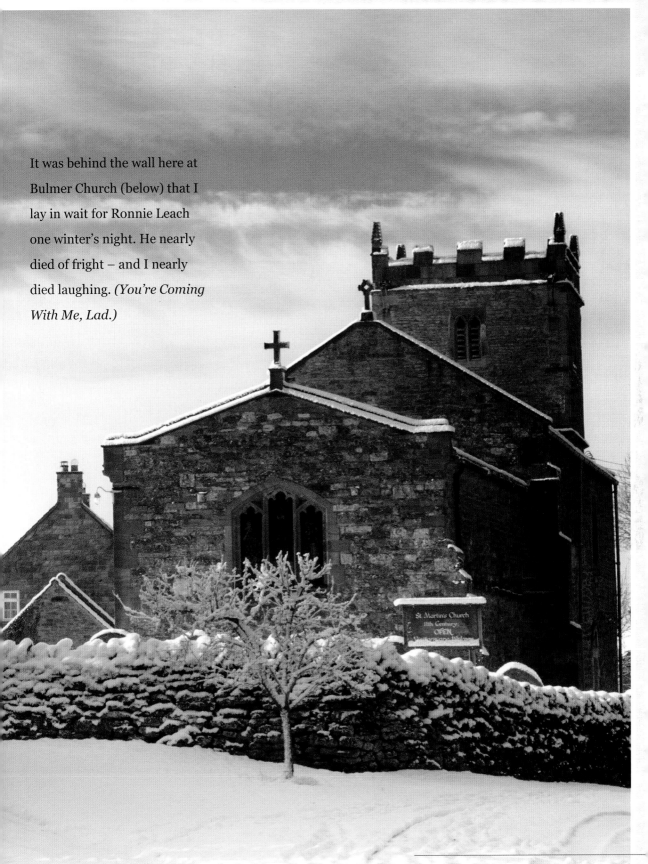

It was behind the wall here at Bulmer Church (below) that I lay in wait for Ronnie Leach one winter's night. He nearly died of fright – and I nearly died laughing. *(You're Coming With Me, Lad.)*

On the Wild Side

I hadn't been at Malton very long when I took on the duties of Wildlife Officer. It's a little-known fact that wildlife crime is second only to drug trafficking in monetary terms. As well as poaching, there's a huge worldwide trade in illegal animal products. So a part of my job was to be aware of the birds and animals that lived in the area – like these deer in Hovingham Woods (facing page), or the hares (facing page top) that attract illegal coursers with dogs. Naturally I had to liaise with the local gamekeepers, quite a few of whom became friends of mine, like Mick Tipping (below).

Badgers, also subject to vicious attacks, are common enough in North Yorkshire, but I'd never seen a little owl until I found an one lying in the road. I took it to a woman we all know as the Badger Lady. She lives in Malton, and takes in all kinds of injured animals. She soon had the patient back on its feet – or wings, I suppose you'd say.

The red kite, recently re-introduced to selected areas and subject to persecution by the odd delinquent landowner.

At the Heart of my Beat

At the very heart of Ryedale, Malton is a traditional market town with Roman origins that attracts shoppers and visitors from miles around. Personally, I don't go in for retail therapy, unless there's food involved – as on market days, or at the annual Food Fair (main photo). And I can never resist free music, especially when it's provided by the White Star Band (below), founded in 1901 and still going strong.

For me, the highlight of the year is the Christmas market. Here, if you know what you're doing, you can pick up a turkey at a bargain price. And if you don't? Well, you'll be none the wiser. This is where I went to buy a turkey for Ann. She'd just been posted to Malton and this was my chance to make an impression. A few days before Christmas she mentioned that she was meant to buy one for her family, but the way her shifts had worked out she would be struggling for time. I was in like Flynn. "Leave it to me," I said. I got her a lovely bird, but I never dared tell her what I paid for it.

A lot of my Country Watch people would show up at Malton market. Many of them were farmers or landowners, and this was a chance to have an informal chat and find out what was on their minds. I might also pick up a few bits of information about poachers operating in the area or indeed livestock rustlers.

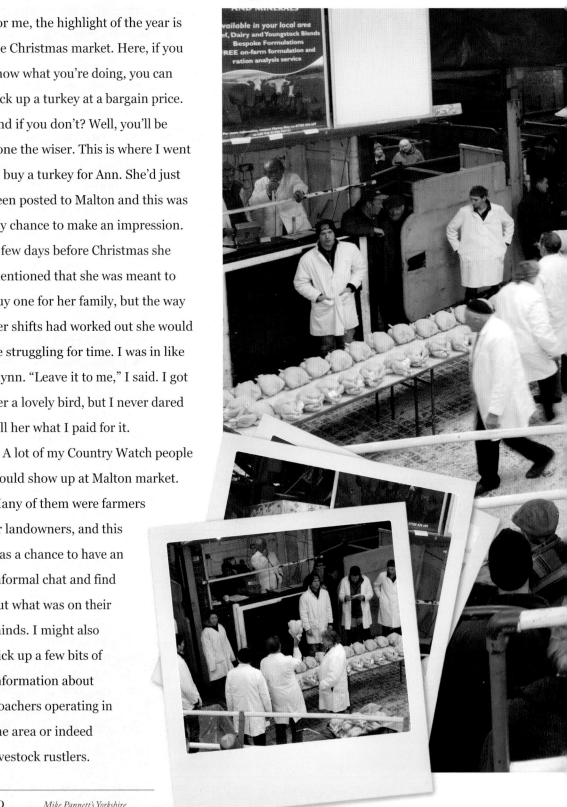

Yates' shop is a Malton institution. All human life is there, you might say. Established over 150 years ago, it sells anything from boots and raincoats to garden and farming implements, nuts and bolts, kitchen pots, pet food, seeds and corn. You can get a ride-on lawnmower, a quad-bike, a yard-brush and pair of wellies – or if you fancy a pig's ear they have a bin of them by the door. Upstairs you can have your bicycle fixed while you get your hair cut. No wonder I was always finding reasons to go in there and chew the fat.

Mike Pannett's Yorkshire

Malton is known around the world as a centre for racehorse training (above). I often stop to watch them on the gallops and have sometimes spotted a likely winner. I just wish the trainers would put their names on them so that I could cash in on a race-day.

Malton Show (right and facing page), held every year in August is a wonderful event that brings together traditional rural activities in the beautiful setting of the Scampston estate.

Out and About

My work took me to every one of Ryedale's villages, and I got to know people in just about all of them. Police work isn't all about chasing the bad guys. A lot of the time we're engaged in preventive work, setting up informal intelligence networks, fostering relationships with older, vulnerable people – and youngsters; and even when there's 'nowt doing' we try to maintain a presence, to 'fly the flag' as we like to say – in other words, making ourselves known to the public we serve. That way, we can help each other.

Sometimes, by way of a change, Ann and I will pop over to Burythorpe for a meal at the Bay Horse (above). I have fond memories of this place – not least the fun we had when Soapy got wed at the little church that stands all alone across the fields, a mile or so from the village (facing page).

If you're observant (and as a copper you have to be) you'll spot some quirky things as you do your rounds, like these wellington boots on a garden fence in Burythorpe.

Even a delightful spot like Hovingham has its share of crime. It was in these woods (main photo), just outside the village, that I lay in wait one icy December night for a gang of turkey thieves who'd been operating in the area. When I stopped a battered old van with three fellows in the front, all covered in feathers, I thought I'd cracked it. How wrong can you be. It turned out they were a gang of pluckers, en route from one job to the next.

It was in the village shop and post office (right) that a gamekeeper's wife was caught up in a raid some years ago. A nasty business.

I do a lot of hiking up in Rosedale – mainly because I love the landscape up there, but also because I know I'll end the day calling in at the New Inn at Cropton (above). This pub flies the Yorkshire flag – and has its own brewery. What more could you want? Grub? They do that too – and it's excellent.

We have some exotic-sounding places in our part of Yorkshire. I was enchanted by Kirby Grindalythe before I ever set eyes on the place, just because of the name. It's derived in part from a Norse word meaning 'valley of the cranes'.

St Mary's at Lastingham is one of my favourite churches. People have worshipped on this site since the late seventh century, and you can still take the narrow staircase down to Britain's only complete Saxon crypt, which lies beneath the 'modern' church, built shortly after the Norman conquest. There's another appealing aspect to the tiny village of Lastingham: the Blacksmith's Arms, just around the corner, right at the foot of the North York Moors.

Like a lot of hikers I've sought shelter in country churchyards, and on occasion inside the church itself. Here are three of my favourites: Whitwell on the Hill, all dressed up for Christmas (main photo);, Kirby Grindalythe, restored by Sir Tatton Sykes in the 1870s (right top), and Thorpe Bassett (right bottom). Both of the latter date back to the twelfth century.

A Place in the Country

We have some grand old country houses on my patch. Say what you like about the people who built up these huge estates, they certainly knew how to make an impression, and they tend to be excellent stewards of the land. On my way home from Malton I'll often take a short detour just to catch a glimpse of Birdsall House, home of the Willoughby family. From there it's a short, steep climb to Leavening Brow and my favourite viewpoint. Two minutes in the car, fifteen on foot. Birdsall itself isn't much of a village. Even the post office is closed now. You might say it never stood much of a chance. When the Willoughbys built the big house in the eighteenth century they decided the village was a bit of an eyesore – so they shifted it half a mile down the hill.

Castle Howard (below), built in the Baroque style and standing in a thousand acres of rolling, landscaped grounds with its own lake (bottom), is the most spectacular example of the English country house within our borders. One of my favourite events here is an outdoor concert, the Last Night of the Proms (facing page), held in the summertime. From a policing angle, who can forget the encounter with the mole that stopped the traffic, as related in *Now Then, Lad*? I never drive by the place without chuckling over that.

One of the great joys of living here is to be able to enjoy the Castle Howard estate in winter, with hardly a visitor in sight (above).

It was along this tree-lined road (right) that I held up the traffic, took off my helmet, and trapped Mister Mole before removing him to safer pastures.

You Mean You Get Paid to Work Here?

When I go back to Battersea and meet up with my old Met colleagues, I like to take a few photos with me and show them my beat. It's called 'rubbing it in'.

In my early days I spent a lot of time at Goathland (below). It was around the time that YTV were filming the Heartbeat series and wanted a police presence. I actually got to know my wife, Ann, when we were on duty up there together. So that was a double bonus: I got to chat with the woman of my dreams while earning double time for working my rest-day. Later we started hiking in the area – as we still do. Park at Levisham, take the train to Goathland (right) and hike back along the valley. I tell that story in *Not On My Patch, Lad*, although I omitted the bit where we made a wide detour around these Highland cattle up on Levisham Moor (following pages).

To me, one of the greatest attractions of the North York Moors is that they have something to offer in all weathers, all seasons. Most people prefer to visit in the summer – especially in July or August when the heather is in bloom. It's certainly a beautiful sight, but I enjoy solitude, and for that you can't beat a quiet winter's day. When they have snow up there it's the real thing. Deep and crisp and even, as the old carol has it. It can be dangerous if you're not properly equipped, of course – but if you're well wrapped up and have your grub, your thermos flask and your foil blanket there are some wonderful hikes to take. This view is taken in Newtondale, towards the end of my favourite walk: Goathland station to Levisham, where you pick up the train to take you back to where you started.

One of my most memorable outings with Ann featured as a story in *Not On My Patch, Lad*. We had a rare day out together and visited the tiny village of Lealholm, where her family come from. We had a gorgeous lunch in the Board Inn (above), then took a short walk across the stepping stones (facing page). After popping into the church we paid a visit to the graveyard (bottom right) where her grandparents are buried.

Helmsley is perhaps the most handsome of the small market towns on my patch. It has a number of luxurious hotels, some fine watering-holes and enough specialist shops to attract visitors all year round.

There are some great walks from here, my favourite being along the path that takes you four miles or so to Rievaulx Abbey (facing page). The only trouble with that one is that there's only one way to get back to town, and that's to re-trace your steps. Still, if you've had a Sunday roast dinner at one of the pubs

it'll help give you an appetite for afternoon tea.

There are also walks to be had around the Duncombe Park estate which borders the town and puts on all kinds of events in the summer months, as well as a Christmas fair.

Helmsley has become a regular meeting-place for the region's many bikers – not the tearaway teenagers of my young day, but well-to-do people in their fifties, sixties and beyond who can finally afford the kind of bike they've always dreamed of. It's great to see people enjoy themselves, and I love to see, and hear, these big beasts in action (I mean the bikes, not the riders!).

Unfortunately there is a down-side. More than once, as I've related in my books, I've had to attend accident scenes involving bikers who have under-estimated the power and speed of their machine – or simply been unlucky. It's a horrible business, especially when there's a fatality involved; and the worst part, after you've sorted out the traffic and gathered the facts, is having to contact the victim's nearest and dearest.

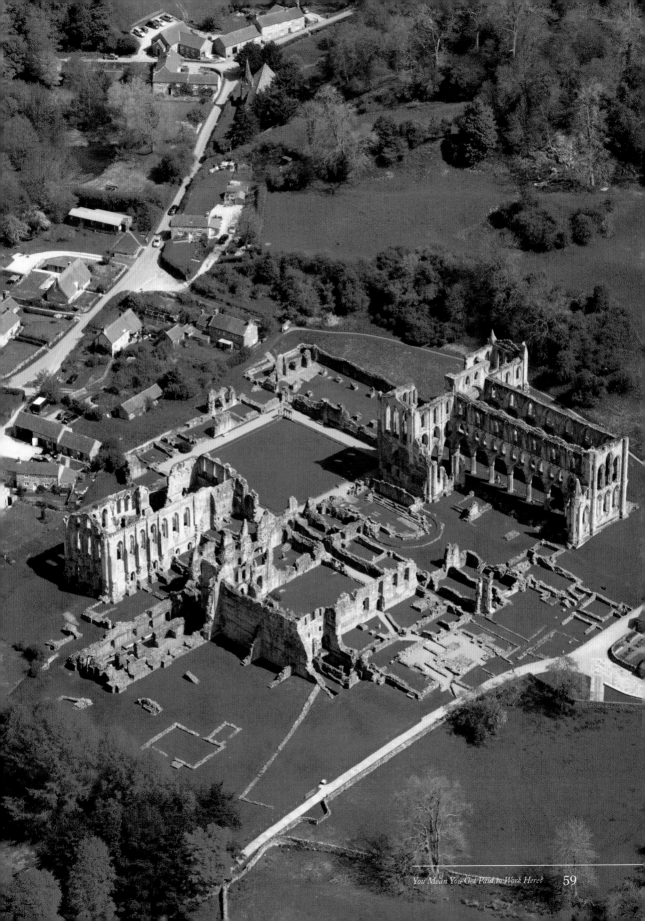

In each of the books about my time as a rural bobby, you'll find there's at least one chapter about an outing of some sort. Call it light relief. I'm one of those people who prides themselves on having a rich and rewarding life away from the job – and there's no better place to relax and refresh your mind and body than North Yorkshire. One of my favourite walks, and it's featured in *Not On My Patch, Lad*, is up to Beck Hole (above) and Mallyan Spout.

At the end of the day, a short drive up to Egton takes you to the Post Gate Inn, and if it's been one of those brisk winter days you'll be glad they put the menus up around that roaring coal fire. By the time you've studied them you'll have thawed out nicely.

Around the Wolds

Many visitors to North Yorkshire get no further than the Moors. Fair enough, it's a beautiful spot, but I really enjoy a day out on the Wolds, not just for the big skies and open fields, but for the villages. Sledmere is right on the edge of my patch. It's an estate village surrounded by traditional parkland (with a replica Eleanor Cross, right), meaning that there is a coherence to its architecture, and a grandeur to the many stands of mature trees. (Facing page, Sledmere's wagoners on parade.)

While Sledmere is beautifully preserved, there's very little left of Wharram Percy (left). The village was abandoned several hundred years ago, most likely due to the depredations of the Black Death, but the remains of the priory and the old lake where the monks raised their fish, tell the tale of a once-thriving community.

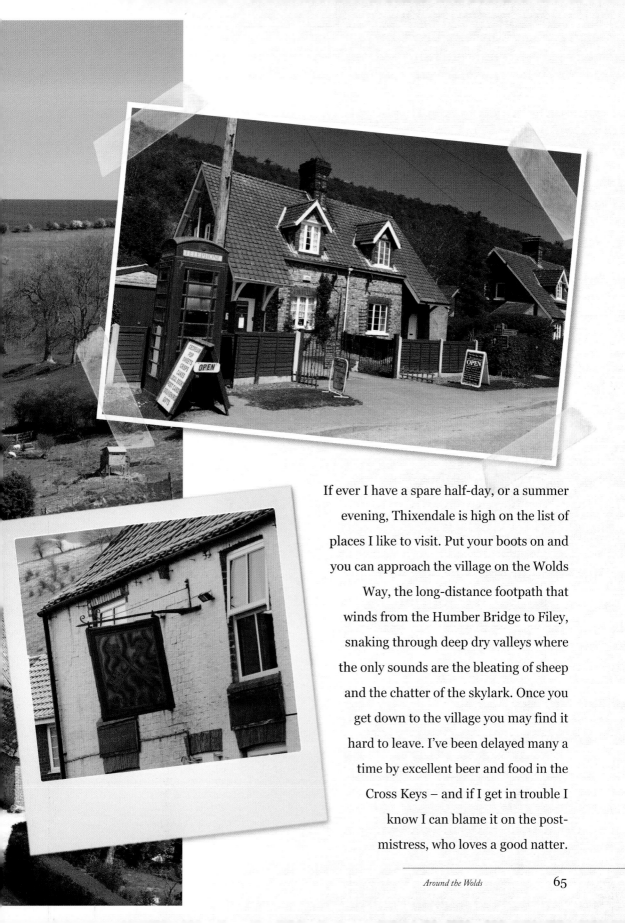

If ever I have a spare half-day, or a summer evening, Thixendale is high on the list of places I like to visit. Put your boots on and you can approach the village on the Wolds Way, the long-distance footpath that winds from the Humber Bridge to Filey, snaking through deep dry valleys where the only sounds are the bleating of sheep and the chatter of the skylark. Once you get down to the village you may find it hard to leave. I've been delayed many a time by excellent beer and food in the Cross Keys – and if I get in trouble I know I can blame it on the post-mistress, who loves a good natter.

Exploring the Vale of York

I spent a lot of time in Crayke in my youth – particularly in the Durham Ox (right). It was one of the stops on my brother's stag night, after we'd done the rounds of village pubs: all the gang in a trailer, pulled by an old grey Fergie with me at the wheel. I'd best not mention the time when a certain daft lad tried to drive his Mini up the front steps … Oh, the foolishness of youth!

The Vale of York is one of those areas where you need to get off the main road and do a bit of exploring. There aren't so many places in England where you can sit and watch a game of cricket with a ruined medieval castle as the back-drop, as you can at Sheriff Hutton (below and main picture); or with a stately home on the boundary, as at Hovingham Hall (below).

At first glance there's not much to Acklam, but it has what every village needs: a church (left) and a pub (below). It was in the Half Moon that we caught two burglars as they emerged from the cellar, their pockets stuffed full of pound coins from the fruit machine.

You couldn't imagine a more idyllic spot than the old bridge across the Derwent at Buttercrambe (facing page). I have occasionally spotted the black swans down there. But a more vivid memory is of the time a farmer called me out. He was halfway across the bridge when he spotted his own Range Rover approaching from the opposite direction, driven by the men who, we later discovered, had just burgled his home.

When the Rivers Rise

The Derwent (opposite page) is a volatile river. It drains a huge swathe of Ryedale between the Moors and the Wolds, and whenever we have a serious downpour we can expect to be on flood alert twenty-four hours later as the run-off comes through Malton. In the main photograph (right), looking downstream from Railway Street, the river is high but not dangerously so. In early November 2000 the bridges here were impassable for several days (below), but fortunately Yates the hardware store put on a tractor and trailer to ferry people across. As soon as word got around, my pal Algy set up in competition!

Fifteen miles away in York, they're well used to the river Ouse rising twelve or thirteen feet – although it's a rare event that sees Cliffords Tower surrounded by water (below).

This is a regular sight along the riverside (right): operatives cleaning up the footpaths, with the Minster in the background.

Farming and Country Pursuits

There's a great tradition of what we call field sports in rural parts, and over recent years, with the legislation about hunting with dogs, the police have been more involved than they used to be. I don't hunt, but I do go rabbiting. I also shoot game birds when I have the chance — strictly for the table — and I do fish. But while I've never participated, I enjoy the sheer spectacle of the hounds, the magnificent horses, and the riders in their red coats. It's a very British scene. Pictured here is Middleton Hunt at Whitwell Hall; and, overleaf, at the Boxing Day hunt in Malton.

The Middleton hounds, looking alert. They're based at Birdsall House.

Above:
Horses at the ready

Left:
One of my favourite sights:
a well-trained dog bringing
home something for the pot.

One of the most enjoyable of my policing duties was working with dogs. Kaizer, pictured here, looks a friendly sort of animal – and if you're behaving yourself you'll come to no harm. However, he's trained to apprehend, chase and capture criminals, and plays a vital role in bringing order to volatile situations. His handler, Ian Squire (top left, next to me), has had him since he was twelve weeks old and trained him since he turned eighteen months to form a unique bond. In 2013 I was privileged to be appointed official Patron of Paws Up, a charity that looks after retired police dogs.

Off Duty

My idea of a perfect day out would be fishing. There's a spot on the Esk, one that very few people know of, where the salmon come up-river in their hundreds. They're a wonderful sight – and they make superb eating.

Facing page:

On a quieter reach of the river, casting a fly. You need immense patience for this business – not something I'm renowned for. But, as my mother always told me, good things come to those who wait ... and wait ... and wait.

Ever since I was a boy and used to walk down to the Scarborough line to talk to the signalman there, I've been fascinated by trains, so of course the North Yorkshire Moors Railway has always been an attraction (right, the line at Levisham). Through my work in promoting the *Now Then, Lad* books I've got to know the folk at the NYMR, and have been privileged to ride behind the legendary number 60007 Sir Nigel Gresley (top, and facing page). Now that's what I call a treat!

Along with my love of railway locomotives goes a fascination with steam engines. I'm a regular visitor to Pickering Traction Engine Rally, which is held every year in August, and, although it's outside my patch, I try to get across to Driffield (above) for their event.

We have a lot of what you'd call spectacular scenery in North Yorkshire, but sometimes a quiet view like this takes my breath away: Bulmer Bank in May, with the trees in leaf and the buttercups in bloom. Magic.

I'd heard of sloe gin, way back from being a youngster, but I thought it was strictly for old codgers. Then I went to live with Walter, who gave me a room when I first came back to Yorkshire and ended up talking his way into the books. He showed me how to make it. It starts with gathering the fruits in October, after they've had a frost on them. Now I'm a convert; or maybe I'm an old codger. (My wife says the jury's out on that.)

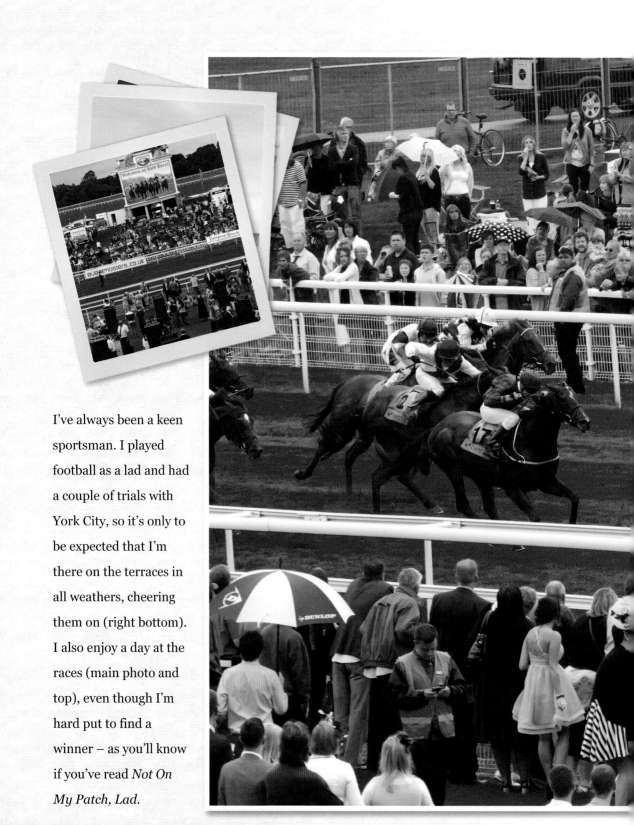

I've always been a keen sportsman. I played football as a lad and had a couple of trials with York City, so it's only to be expected that I'm there on the terraces in all weathers, cheering them on (right bottom). I also enjoy a day at the races (main photo and top), even though I'm hard put to find a winner – as you'll know if you've read *Not On My Patch, Lad*.

I've mentioned the time I spent at Staintondale (top) as a lad –
and there'll be more of that when I write the story of my
childhood. One of the big treats when we went away was to
drive into Scarborough (main picture) for fish and chips.
My favourite seaside resort, though, has to be Whitby (above),
narrow streets, the macabre associations with Count Dracula,
and of course the famous fish suppers. You can't beat 'em.

A trip to the Dales

You still meet people in Yorkshire who've never been outside of our fair county. I know one old boy, up near Levisham, who's never been outside the North Riding, apart from a trip to hospital in Leeds – and his verdict on that adventure was that he won't be trying it again in a hurry. "Why, the buggers had me appendix out," he said. And he sounded genuinely aggrieved. But when I say that I like to have a change of scene and take myself off to the Dales, it doesn't mean I don't travel abroad when I can afford it, just that I'm not blind to the appeal of that part of Yorkshire.

There's a passage in *You're coming With Me, Lad* where I'm standing admiring my friend Algy's MG sports car. I'd been getting to know Ann and really wanted to invite her on a date – but where? As a PC dating a sergeant, I had to be discreet: that sort of thing was frowned upon. Algy had the answer:

"These cars are like animals. They need exercising. I was going to take the little MG out last week, but the blasted battery failed on me." He hesitated. "I mean, you and this – what did you say her name was?"

"Ann."

"Ah yes, lovely girl! You and Ann... you like the occasional trip out, I presume?"

"Oh, hell aye. It's just that we have to be careful not to be seen in this neck of the woods."

"Perfect." He tapped the side of his head. "This is where the Algernon brainwave... kicks in, as they put it. What would you say to taking the MG here for a run? It needs a bit of a blow-through. Clean out the valves and so on." He flicked his cloth over the radiator grille. "Been parked here all winter gathering dust, and I dare say the old exhaust is clogged with soot."

"I'd love to, but – are you sure?"

"Of course I'm sure, old chum. You'll be doing me a favour. In fact, have her for the weekend. Take the young lady out to the Dales and find yourselves a nice hotel somewhere."

"Algy, I'm going to say yes before you change your mind. No idea when we'll manage a weekend off together, of course, but leave it with me."

"Splendid."

If you've read *You're Coming With Me, Lad* you'll remember that Ann and I have a friend with a

sports car....

When Ann and I had our day out in Algy's MG we headed for Wharfedale. Our base was to be Kettlewell (facing page, seen from the moor). We took our time, as you need to over there – the scenery is so magnificent – and stopped for a picnic lunch beside Grimwith Reservoir (above). It was getting cool, and, being a true gentleman, I lent Ann my leather flying jacket.

Mind you, the weather got a lot worse on the way home. We ran into a full-blown thunderstorm and couldn't get the top on. We limped along with three inches of water on the floor between us. But who cares about a bit of a soaking when you're in love?

We took in trips to Grassington for the farmers' market (below); and also explored nearby Nidderdale and the market town of Pateley Bridge (right, seen from the moor), home of the famous Nidderdale Show (above).

Having invited Ann to go to the Dales with me, I hesitated to throw in a trip to the trout farm at Kilnsey Crag, but she smiled sweetly and said it would be okay so long as I caught something to take home. I got a beauty – although we didn't eat it that night. Instead, we stopped at Betty's tea-room in Harrogate (above) on the way home.

When the Mood Takes Me

Working as a policeman brings you in touch with all kinds of people – and all their many facets, both heart-warming and chilling. It takes a lot out of you, and from time to time you just want to get away, on your own, and re-charge your batteries. I'll often take the dog up to Sutton Bank (above), from where you can see half of our great county spread out, with Gormire Lake just below you (right). Or I'll go up to Rosedale and walk Spaunton Moor to Ana Cross (inset).

Our countryside is so varied – from the gentle slopes of the Howardian Hills near Yearsley (above) to the heights of Sutton Bank and this fantastic view over the Vale of York.

Rosedale (facing page) is my favourite of the valleys that divide the North York Moors. When you stand there surrounded by the heather and look down on lush green valleys below (right), it's hard to imagine that was the site of an industrial boom a mere century ago. But the workings of the old iron ore mines are still very visible in places (above).

Being a copper means working shifts, and that can be disruptive if you've a family. But there are compensations, like driving back to the nick after a busy night shift and seeing the dawn break along the Yearsley to Hovingham road.

Reflective Moments

Being out and about in the countryside every day you become much more aware of the seasons, and better able to enjoy each one in turn. When I lived in London I didn't like winter. It was gloomy, wet and cold. I was always waiting, impatiently, for summer to come. In Yorkshire, if you wrap up warm, there's something to enjoy in all weathers. I've got into the habit of doing what we did when we were children: standing and watching, absorbing every detail, winter and summer, and being thankful for what I see.

We have a lot of wooded land around us, and I've become much more aware of the great variety of colours and textures to be found in the various trees. Everything from the newly-sprung seeds on a young ash tree to the rich autumn colours of leaves scattered on the forest floor.

There's no getting away from sheep in our part of the world – not even along the main street of Hutton le Hole where they graze the sides of the beck and keep the greens trimmed.

Ryedale, of course, is all about farming – and the farmers always seem to be at work. When they're not, they're waiting for the weather to change so that that they can get to work – or complaining about it! From autumn ploughing, to spring planting to harvest, I love to see the seasons unfold. Mind you, my father had another way of putting that. He used to say, I love work: I can stand and look at it all day. Here they are gathering silage under the shadow of one of our most recognisable landmarks: the White Horse of Kilburn.

If you stand around for long enough, you can guarantee that you'll soon gather a few inquisitive cows around you. These gentle beasts are at Hanging Grimston, a couple of miles south of Leavening.

Perhaps my favourite walk, when I've been feeling the strain, is along the Cleveland Way. That's the long-distance footpath that starts at Helmsley and takes you up to Sutton Bank, then follows the outline of the Moors all the way to the coast at Scarborough (right) and on to Filey.

When I was a lad, I seem to remember that we had to go out to the coast to see a seagull. Nowadays there seem to be more and more of them inland, following the plough. Better pickings, I suppose.

I once had a friend up from London. We were out walking when a cock pheasant got up, right in front of us, with the usual squawking and flapping. Frightened the life out of him. He'd never seen a live one. I told him to watch where he was treading or he'd most likely scare up another one.

I'm not a huge fan of poetry, but I always remember one we had to read at school: 'Stopping by woods on a snowy evening' by Robert Frost. It's the sort of thing that comes to mind when you're out and about in the wintertime.

There's a sort of ghostliness comes over the woods when the first snow has fallen. Once in a while I'll remember to stop and allow it to wash over me.

When winter comes to North Yorkshire it can be severe. I've had to work alongside Scarborough & Ryedale Mountain Rescue team on several occasions, and have never failed to be struck by their skill, commitment and dedication. A fantastic bunch of lads and lasses.

Acknowledgements

Mike Pannett: I would like to say a huge thank you to my beautiful wife Ann, and to all my family and friends. They have supported me tirelessly over the past few years whilst I have written and promoted my series of Yorkshire policing books. To the entire policing family, who in my opinion are simply the 'Best in the world'. It is often not an easy job, and sometimes things don't go to plan. But what is never really ever reported on is the fact that the majority of the time they do outstanding and difficult work.

Alan Wilkinson must get a special mention. I have worked closely with Alan for many years now on all my books. Without him, the books would not be the same. Alan and I share a number of passions: the countryside and walking, as well as the enjoyment of conversation over a good pint. *www.alan-wilkinson.com*

What a pleasure it has been working closely with John Potter over the past year. He has been out in all weathers and at varied locations in order to capture all of the four seasons. I think I could write another book about it! He's a great character, and his work speaks for itself.

John Potter: I would like to thank the following people and organisations for helping me with this project: Duncombe Park, near Helmsley, and in particular Graham Mee who helped me to photograph hares *(www.duncombepark.com)*; Mick Tipping, gamekeeper, now retired, who gave me some very useful advice and contacts; Steve Clay, gamekeeper on the Hovingham Estate; Scarborough and Ryedale Mountain Rescue Team, and in particular Ian Hugill – working with the team in midwinter in Dalby Forest under heavy snow was amazing *(www.srmrt.org.uk)*; Middleton Hunt for inviting me to the kennels at Birdsall and then to several of their meetings *(www.middletonhunt.co.uk)*; St Michael's Church, Market Place, Malton, and especially the churchwarden John Rummel who allowed me and a photographer friend to work from the tower during Malton Food Lovers Festival *(www.stmichaelsmalton.org.uk)*.

Useful information

Readers from all over the world and people I meet often ask me about Yorkshire — where and when to visit, where to stay, and so on. Here are some useful organisations:

Welcome to Yorkshire: www.yorkshire.com
Visit York: www.visityork.org
North Yorkshire Moors Railway: www.nymr.co.uk
Black Sheep Brewery: www.blacksheepbrewery.com
Grand Central: www.grandcentralrail.com
Bettys Café Tea Rooms & Yorkshire Tea: www.bettysandtaylors.co.uk

With thanks for continued support and great brews

I am also a huge supporter of the people you might need one day. The local mountain and cave rescue teams all do a great job. They're highly skilled volunteers who go out in all weathers looking out for each and every one of us. This service depends on donations for fuel and equipment, so please suppor their work!

www.srmrt.org.uk
www.swaledalemrt.org.uk
www.csrt.co.uk
www.cro.org.uk
www.uwfra.org.uk

I have recently become the patron of the retired police dog benevolent charity PawsUpUK. This is a new charity which I hope will grow as time progresses. It is a huge honour for me to be asked to take on the role for this vital charity caring for our retired working dogs.

www.pawsup.org.uk

And finally...

If you would like to contact me for speaking engagements or to meet me at events, please visit my website for details *www.mikepannett.co.uk*.